THE BIG 5: AFRICAN SAFARI ANIMALS

CAPE BUFFALO

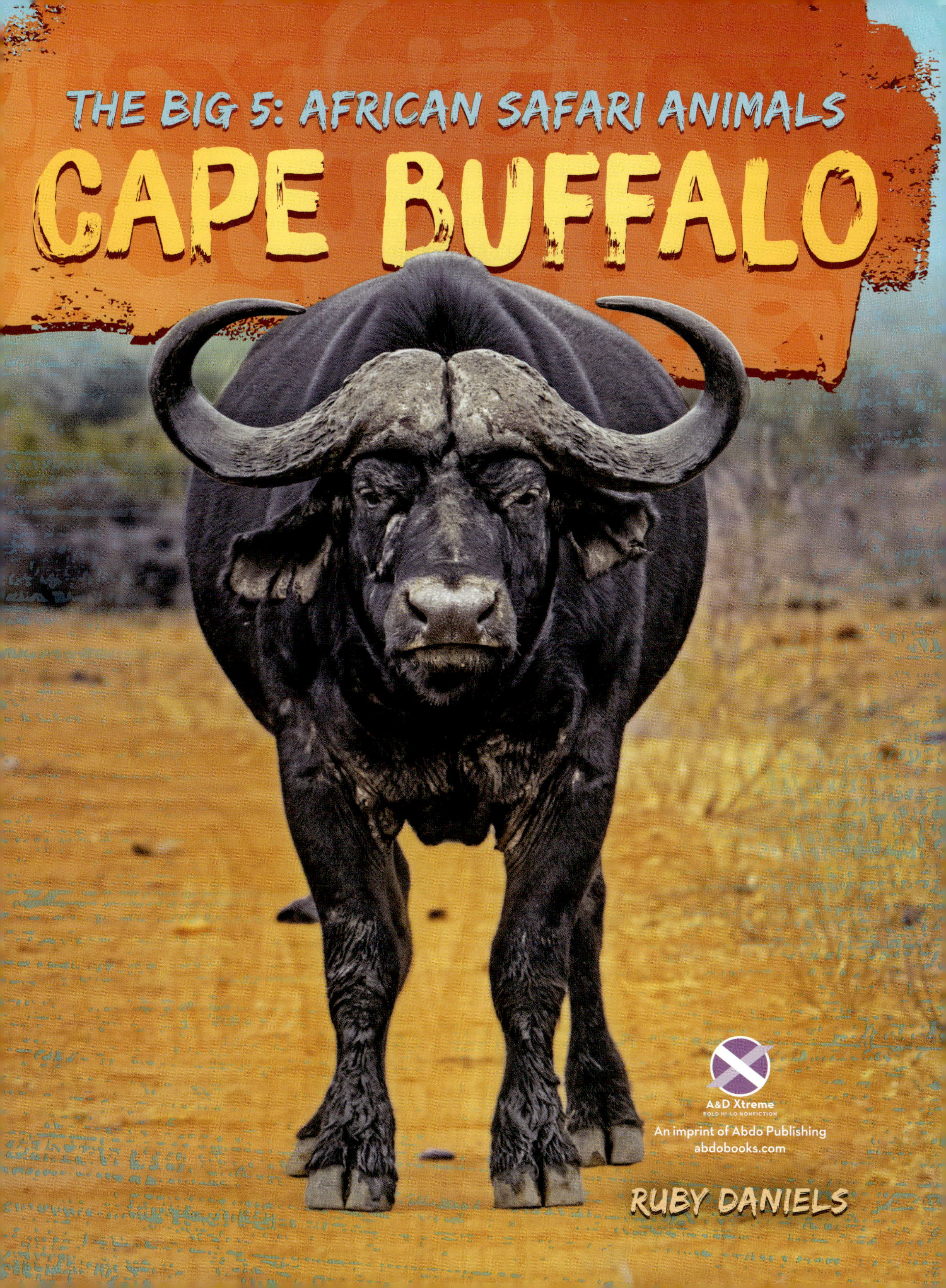

A&D Xtreme

An imprint of Abdo Publishing
abdobooks.com

RUBY DANIELS

TAKE IT TO THE XTREME!

GET READY FOR AN EXTREME ADVENTURE! THE PAGES OF THIS BOOK WILL TAKE YOU INTO THE THRILLING WORLD OF ICONIC AFRICAN ANIMALS. WHEN YOU HAVE FINISHED READING THIS BOOK, TAKE THE XTREME CHALLENGE ON PAGE 45 ABOUT WHAT YOU'VE LEARNED!

ABDOBOOKS.COM
Published by Abdo Publishing, a division of ABDO, PO Box 398166, Minneapolis, Minnesota 55439.

Printed in the United States of America, North Mankato, MN.
052025
092025

THIS BOOK CONTAINS RECYCLED MATERIALS

Design: Kelly Doudna, Mighty Media, Inc.
Production: Mighty Media, Inc.
Editor: Katherine Chu

Cover Photograph: Anna-Carina Nagel/iStockphoto

Interior Photographs: Albert Beukhof/Shutterstock, pp. 42–43; AndreAnita/Shutterstock, pp. 14–15; Anna-Carina Nagel/iStockphoto, p. 1; Bob Pool/Shutterstock, pp. 30–31; David Havel/Shutterstock, pp. 38–39; FOTOGRIN/Shutterstock, pp. 4–5; Hannes Thirion/Shutterstock, pp. 8–9; henk bogaard/Adobe Stock pp. 24–25; Henk Bogaard/iStockphoto, p. 23; Holly Auchincloss/Shutterstock, pp. 32–33; Jane Rix/Shutterstock, pp. 22–23; Lyle Gregg/Shutterstock, pp. 40–41; Marc_H/Shutterstock, pp. 34–35; Marion Smith-Byers/Shutterstock, pp. 26–27; Martin Prochazkacz, pp. 18–19; Noppe Herlinde/Shutterstock, pp. 6–7; nwdph/Shutterstock, pp. 10–11; PACO COMO/Adobe Stock, p. 44; PACO COMO/Shutterstock, pp. 28–29; Papa Bravo/Shutterstock, pp. 16–17; Photography Phor Phun/Shutterstock, pp. 12–13; Vlad Karavaev/Shutterstock, pp. 36–37; Yongyut Kumsri/Shutterstock, pp. 20–21

Design Elements: DGIM studio/Adobe Stock (distressed texture); Ografica/Adobe Stock (header background); Zebra Finch/Adobe Stock (header background)

LIBRARY OF CONGRESS CONTROL NUMBER: 2024948545
PUBLISHER'S CATALOGING-IN-PUBLICATION DATA
Names: Daniels, Ruby, author.
Title: Cape buffalo / by Ruby Daniels
Description: Minneapolis, Minnesota : Abdo Publishing, 2026 | Series: The big 5: African safari animals | Includes online resources and index.
Identifiers: ISBN 9781098296308 (lib. bdg.) | ISBN 9798384917731 (ebook)
Subjects: LCSH: Cape buffalo--Juvenile literature. | African buffalo--Juvenile literature. | Big game animals--Africa--Juvenile literature. | Herbivores--Juvenile literature. | Safaris--Juvenile literature.
Classification: DDC 591.96--dc23

CONTENTS

CHAPTER 1

CAPE BUFFALO CRUISE

Adult Cape buffalo are usually dark gray or black. Cape buffalo calves are typically reddish brown.

While on a safari in Tanzania, you notice hundreds of dark shapes in the distance. As you get closer, you see they are big creatures with large horns. You hear snorts, bellows, and cow-like grunts. You've just spotted a herd of Cape buffalo!

CHAPTER 2

PART OF THE BIG 5

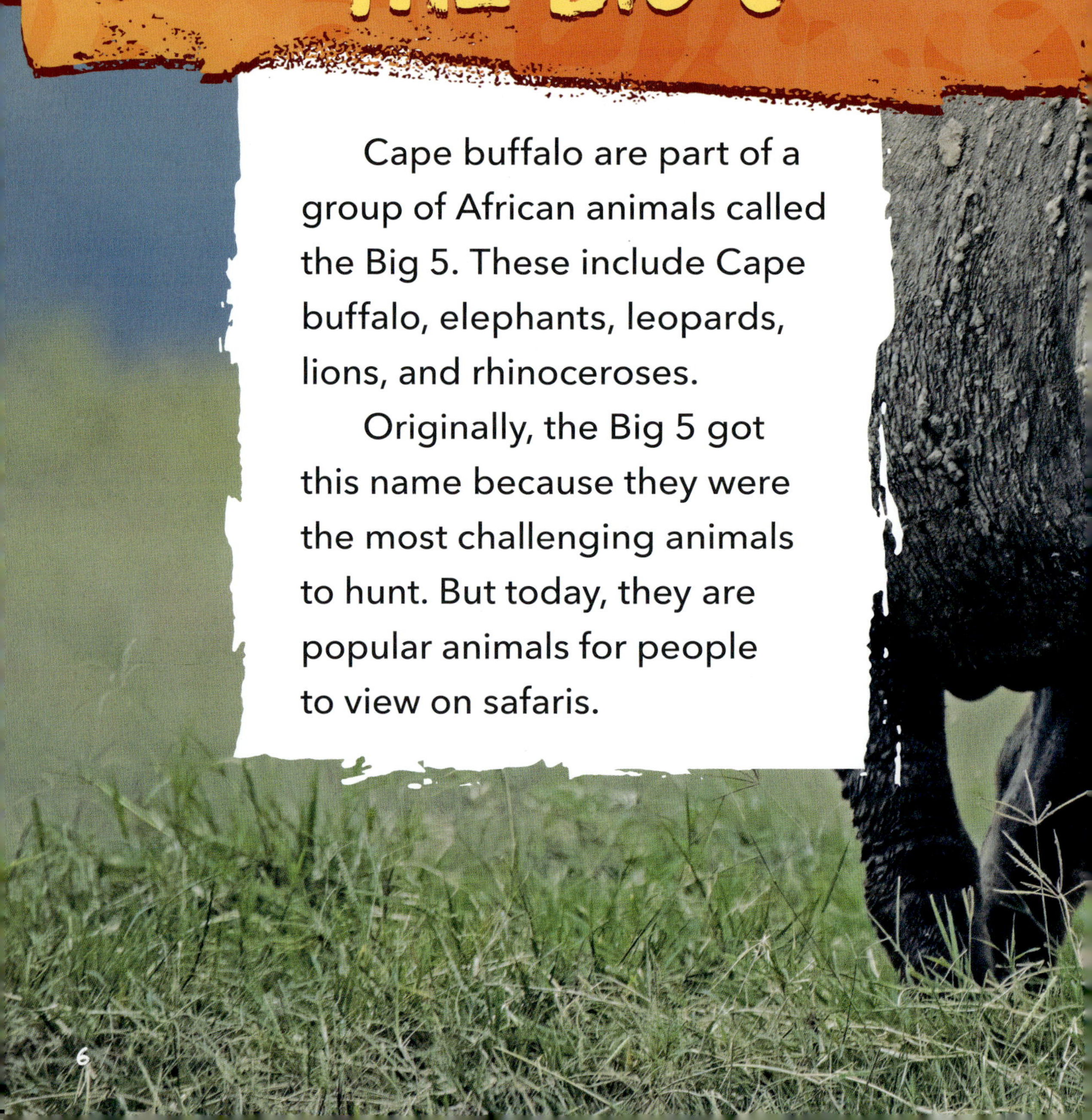

Cape buffalo are part of a group of African animals called the Big 5. These include Cape buffalo, elephants, leopards, lions, and rhinoceroses.

Originally, the Big 5 got this name because they were the most challenging animals to hunt. But today, they are popular animals for people to view on safaris.

Cape buffalo are also known as African buffalo.

CHAPTER 3

THE CAPE BUFFALO

The Cape buffalo is the largest wild **bovid** in Africa. It only reaches about five feet (1.5 m) tall at the shoulder. Yet it can weigh up to 1,900 pounds (862 kg). That's almost one ton (0.9 t)!

XTREME FACT

Some people call bison buffalo. Bison are also bovids, but they are not buffalo.

An ungulate is a type of mammal that has hooves. This makes the Cape buffalo an ungulate.

A Cape buffalo's diet is mostly grass. If there is not any grass available, Cape buffalo will eat woody plants.

Cape buffalo are ruminants. These are even-toed hoofed **mammals** that chew **cud**. A Cape buffalo's stomach has four closed spaces or chambers. These help the buffalo process any grass it eats.

The first chamber softens and turns grass into cud. After it has softened, the buffalo brings the cud back up to its mouth and rechews it. The cud is then broken down into **nutrients** in the other three stomach chambers.

Cape buffalo have two large, curved horns. An adult male's horns meet on the forehead. This makes its horns look like a helmet. A female's horns are smaller and narrower. Cape buffalo use their horns to fight, charge predators, and **defend** themselves.

The bottom of a male Cape buffalo's horns join together to make a hard shield called a boss.

CHAPTER 4

LIFE BY THE WATER

Cape buffalo live around 11 to 22 years in the wild.

Cape buffalo mainly live in regions south of the African Sahara Desert. They can live in a wide range of **habitats**. These include grasslands, bushlands, dry **savannas**, and even swamps. They just need grass to eat and water to drink to survive.

XTREME FACT

Cape buffalo are always within a day's walk of a water source.

Cape buffalo usually live in herds. Each herd has about 50 to 500 male and female buffalo. Living in large groups helps protect buffalo from predators. It means the buffalo can **defend** each other.

Younger male buffalo will push older males out of their herd. These older buffalo live together in small all-male herds or on their own.

XTREME FACT

During the dry season, Cape buffalo can gather in the Serengeti in groups of more than 1,000 buffalo!

Buffalo calves completely depend on their mother for at least one year.

Females have calves about every two years. Their **gestation** period is 11 to 12 months long. They usually give birth at the end of the rainy season. This means there is more grass for the mothers to eat so they can make milk for their calves.

XTREME FACT

Female buffalo stay in the same herd throughout their lifetime. Male buffalo leave their herd at about age four.

Cape buffalo communicate using vocal calls and body language. Calves grunt or bleat when scared, playing, or calling for their mother. Males use certain body positions to show **dominance** and submission.

Male Cape buffalo also fight to determine dominance. The dominant males get to mate with female buffalo.

Cape buffalo even vote as a herd on which way to go. While the herd is resting, individual buffalo will stand up and stare in the direction they want to go. Then they lie back down. When the resting period ends, the group goes in the direction most voted on.

CHAPTER 5

CAPE BUFFALO UNDER THREAT

Cape buffalo are near threatened. This means the **species** is likely to qualify as threatened in the **future**. Cape buffalo face many threats. These include natural threats, **habitat** loss and fragmentation, poaching, and human-buffalo conflict.

Though Cape buffalo are not in danger of becoming extinct, researchers found buffalo numbers have been decreasing for decades.

According to the International Union for Conservation of Nature, there are fewer than 401,000 Cape buffalo left on Earth.

Cape buffalo are natural prey. Lions, leopards, hyenas, and wild dogs hunt and eat buffalo. So, buffalo must fight or avoid these animals to survive.

Droughts and **diseases** are also natural threats to Cape buffalo. Droughts create less food and can cause **starvation**. Diseases can spread quickly and kill many Cape buffalo.

XTREME FACT

A rinderpest plague killed up to 90 percent of the buffalo in Africa in the 1890s. Scientists consider it to be one of the deadliest cattle diseases. Scientists created a vaccine that destroyed the disease by 2011.

Cape buffalo have very thick skin. This helps protect them during an attack.

Human activity is the main cause of **habitat** loss and fragmentation. Habitat loss is when the size of an animal's habitat is reduced. Habitat fragmentation is when an animal's habitat is broken up. Both result in less land for buffalo to survive on.

Poaching is illegal hunting. Some people poach wild animals such as Cape buffalo for their meat. This is called **bushmeat** hunting. This kills buffalo faster than they can reproduce.

Livestock take up much of the grazing land buffalo need.

People see buffalo as dangerous. This is because of how fast and easily buffalo attack when they feel threatened.

Problems can occur when Cape buffalo and humans live near each other. Cape buffalo are large and powerful animals. They can break fences, destroy crops, and spread **disease** to livestock. So, farmers may kill buffalo to protect their farms and livestock. This is called human-buffalo conflict.

CHAPTER 6

ESSENTIAL ANIMALS

The loss of Cape buffalo is a serious issue. They are important for the survival of other **species** in their **ecosystem**. Buffalo eat the tall, rough grasses that smaller animals cannot **digest**.

Clearing the taller grass also means smaller animals can reach the shorter grasses they need.

Cape buffalo also help certain birds survive. These birds perch on buffalo and eat the bugs that land on them. Birds also ride the buffalo to different areas.

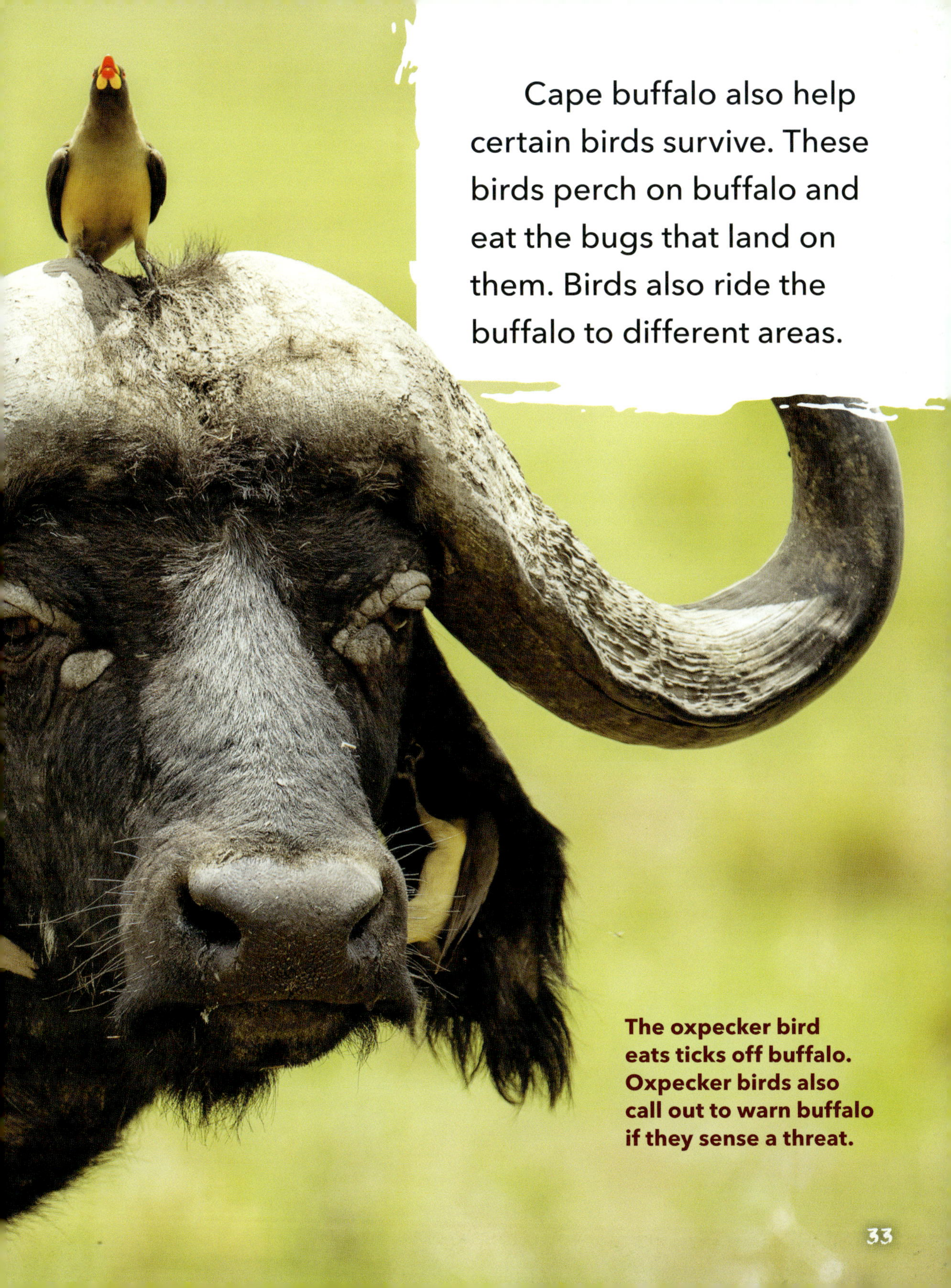

The oxpecker bird eats ticks off buffalo. Oxpecker birds also call out to warn buffalo if they sense a threat.

CHAPTER 7

HELP IS ON THE WAY

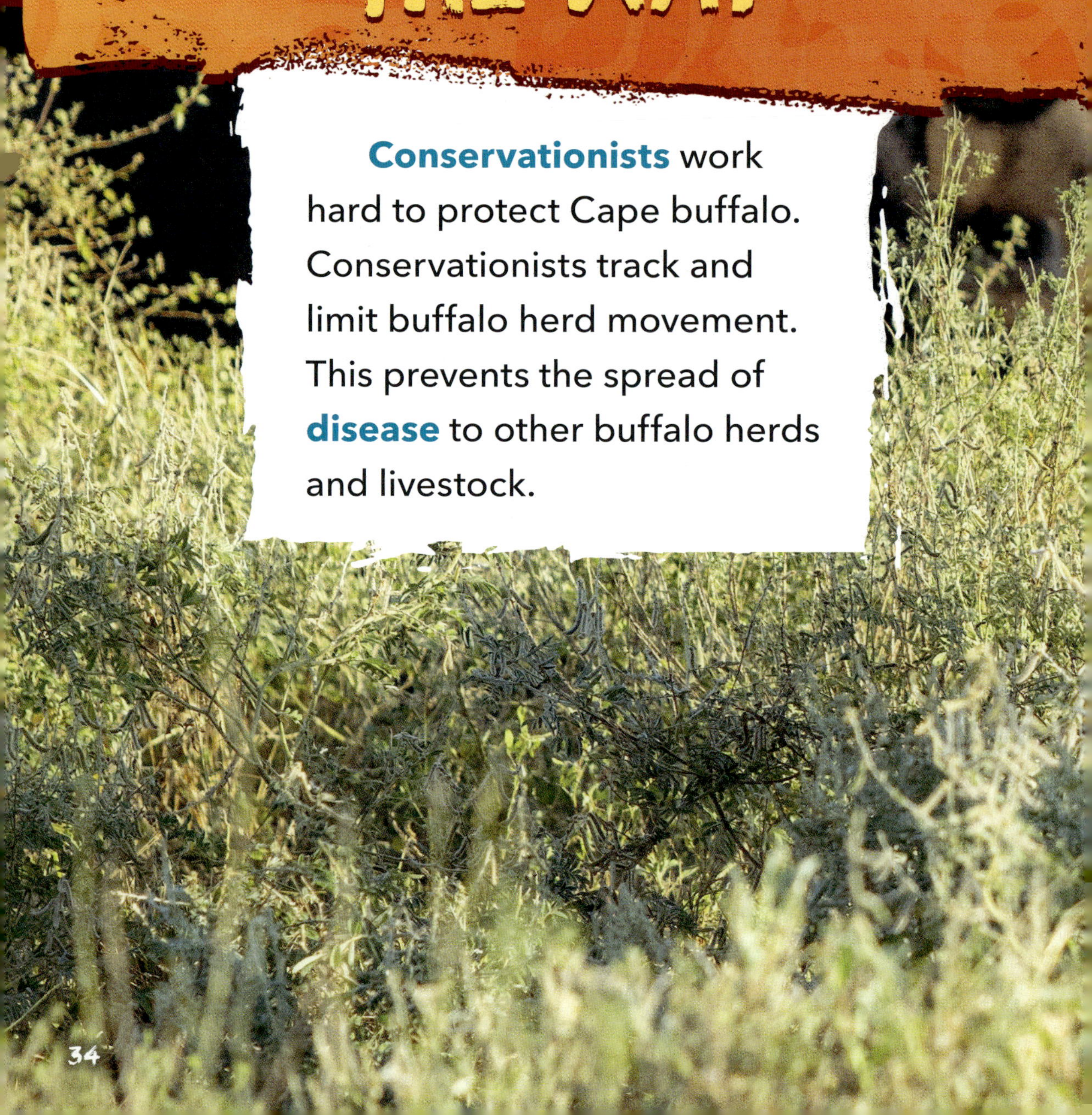

Conservationists work hard to protect Cape buffalo. Conservationists track and limit buffalo herd movement. This prevents the spread of **disease** to other buffalo herds and livestock.

Organizations make sure buffalo are free from disease before introducing them to wildlife preserves.

Farm Africa is an organization that helps African farmers grow healthier crops. It also helps farmers find ways to sell their crops for more money.

Other **conservationists** try to prevent **habitat** loss and fragmentation. Some organizations work with different countries' governments when they plan new buildings and systems. The organizations make sure these projects affect buffalo populations as little as possible.

Some organizations also work with communities. They teach people farming methods that use less land. This leaves more space for Cape buffalo to roam.

Some organizations try to reduce human-buffalo conflict. For example, if a hostile buffalo lives close to humans, the organization will move it to a wildlife preserve. **Conservationists** also educate communities.

Conservationists move buffalo to new locations for many reasons. These can include creating new herds in areas where there aren't any buffalo, mixing populations, and preventing human-buffalo conflict.

They recommend blocking off areas of land around the parks where Cape buffalo live. This provides more space between the buffalo and farms. And **conservationists** suggest not growing crops near buffalo **habitats**.

CHAPTER 8

FAN FAVORITES

Cape buffalo are popular animals to view on African safaris. They are unusual and splendid animals. Buffalo gather in very large groups. So they are usually easy to spot. People on safari may see herds moving together or **defending** themselves against a lion attack. They may even see a buffalo charging!

XTREME FACT

Cape buffalo can charge at speeds of more than 35 miles per hour (56.3 kmh)!

When threatened, herds will create a circle around weak herd members. Strong males will face out and defend against predators.

People on safari might also see Cape buffalo taking a mud bath. This helps buffalo cool down and protects them from pests.

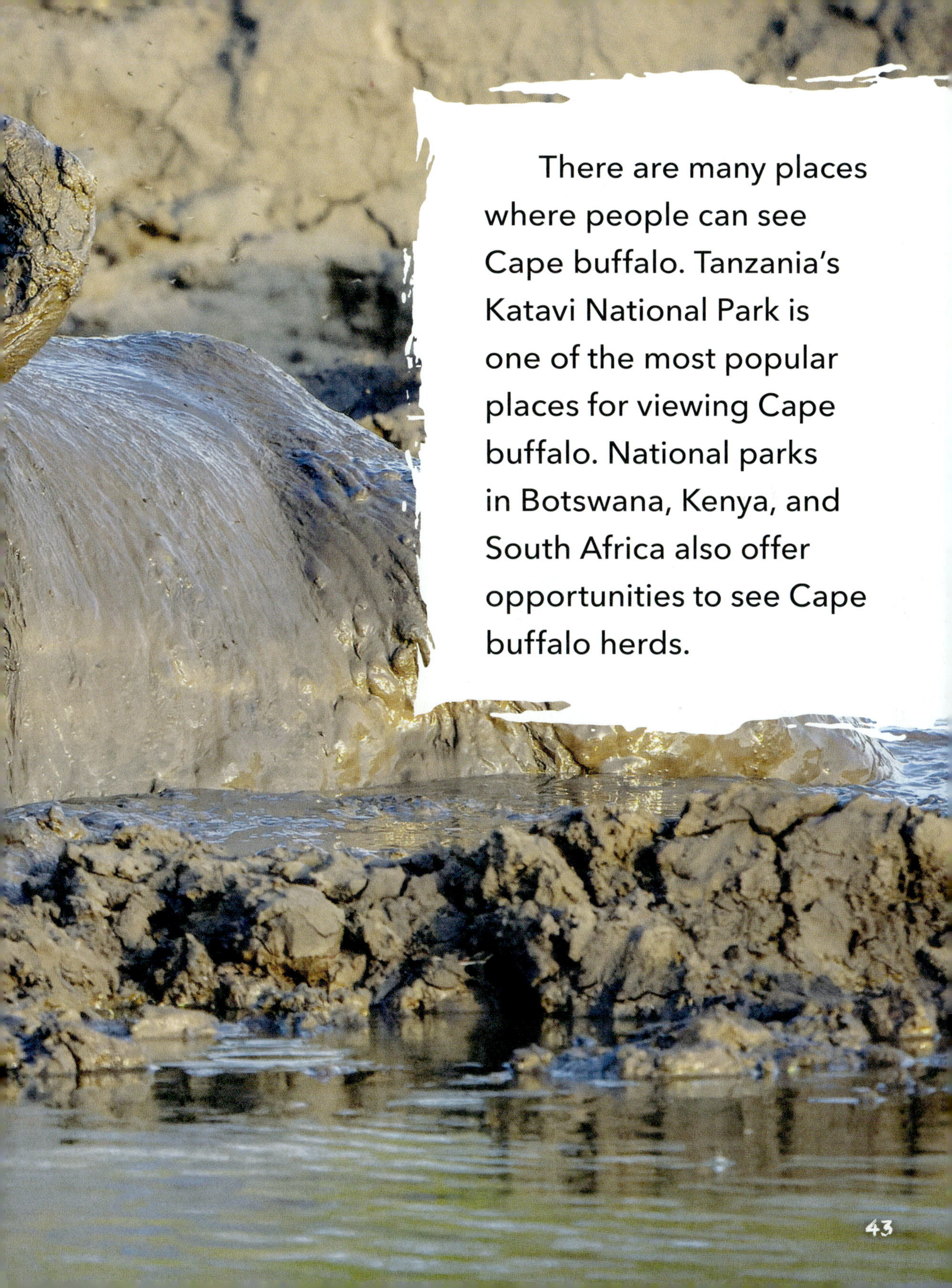

There are many places where people can see Cape buffalo. Tanzania's Katavi National Park is one of the most popular places for viewing Cape buffalo. National parks in Botswana, Kenya, and South Africa also offer opportunities to see Cape buffalo herds.

CHAPTER 9

MORE TO EXPLORE

Cape buffalo are remarkable animals. Their size, enormous herds, and horns make them interesting. Though Cape buffalo face many threats, **conservationists** work hard to preserve their **habitats** and protect them. Animal lovers can go on a wildlife safari and enjoy these wonderful creatures in their natural habitats.

Cape buffalo calves can stand and start to walk as soon as ten minutes after being born.

XTREME CHALLENGE

TAKE THE QUIZ BELOW AND PUT WHAT YOU'VE LEARNED TO THE TEST!

1) What qualities make Cape buffalo unusual?

2) Why do Cape buffalo live in herds?

3) What causes human-buffalo conflict?

4) How does the size and location of farmland affect Cape buffalo?

5) Would you want to see Cape buffalo on a safari? Why or why not?

GLOSSARY

bovid–any animal in the Bovidae family. This is a family of ruminants that have two hollow, permanently attached horns that do not branch out.

bushmeat–meat that comes from hunting wild animals.

conservation–the planned management of natural resources or animals to protect them from damage or destruction. People who do this are conservationists.

cud–food brought back into the mouth from the stomach to be chewed again.

defend–to protect from harm or attack.

digest–to break down food into simpler substances that the body can absorb.

disease–a sickness.

dominance–having power or importance over others.

drought–a long period of dry weather.

ecosystem–a community of organisms and their surroundings.

future–a time that has not yet occurred.

gestation–the carrying of a developing unborn baby in the uterus.

habitat—a place where a living thing is naturally found.

mammal—a warm-blooded animal that has hair and whose females produce milk to feed their young.

nutrient—a substance found in food and used in the body. Nutrients help the body grow, stay healthy, and repair itself.

rinderpest plague—a sickness caused by a virus that is likely to spread and cause death to cloven-hoofed animals.

savanna—a grassy plain with few or no trees.

species—a group of related living beings that can naturally produce offspring with each other.

starvation—the act of suffering or death from lack of food.

ONLINE RESOURCES

Booklinks
NONFICTION NETWORK
FREE! ONLINE NONFICTION RESOURCES

To learn more about African Cape buffalo, please visit **abdobooklinks.com** or scan this QR code. These links are routinely monitored and updated to provide the most current information available.

INDEX